ON INVESTING WELL

THE ELEMENTS OF GOOD INVESTING

Printed in the United States of America
First Printing 2019

ISBN: 978-17339648-0-7

Cover designed by Kelsey Remy Illustration & Design, www.kelseyremy.com

To contact the author, visit:
www.huntcountryinvestments.com
advisor@huntcountryinvestments.com

CONTENTS

PART III

Methods **65**

Appendixes...**83**

About the Author..**99**

AUTHOR'S FOREWORD

"Out of clutter, find simplicity."

—Albert Einstein

Albert Einstein—physicist, philosopher and the developer of the theory of relativity—was not talking about investing when he said this. Yet his imperative applies to investing today.

Investing and financial planning have become overly complex. We have more tools but less knowledge. We have more information but less understanding. We have more experts but less wisdom.

Of course, we live in a complex world and the financial markets are by nature complicated.

But in the face of this inherent complexity, I believe the key to successful investing is quite simple. We need only to shift our mindsets, learn sound principles and use proven methods.

Achieving simplicity in investing through those three actions can yield great financial success. Doing so, however, requires hard work and discipline.

So let's get started.

INTRODUCTION

T he United States is entering an *Era of Personal Responsibility*. Traditionally, employers and the government have shouldered the responsibility of saving and paying for citizens' college, health care and retirement.

FIG 1.1 THE OLD SYSTEM

But now, both institutions which have traditionally been responsible for ensuring the financial security of the general population have pushed it back onto the people.

FIG 1.2 THE NEW SYSTEM

No longer can you work for the same company for 40 years and retire with a generous pension. When you eventually retire—if you are able to—you are likely to find Social Security is underfunded, unsustainable or even insolvent.

In this new system, you bear most of the burden for saving for your college education, health care and retirement. If you want to survive and thrive in this *Era of Personal Responsibility*, it is up to you to make it happen. No one else is going to do it for you.

Knowing how to properly invest and build your own wealth is a vital skill to succeed in this new age. Our education system, however, does not teach how to invest well, and most of the available material on investing is unhelpful, inaccurate or confusing.

This book is an attempt to cut a clear path through the vast jungle of investing information. You will not find it to be a list of rules on what to do and what not to do or a prescription for exactly how you should invest.

Instead, you will find the following chapters present in a simple and useful manner the mindsets, principles and methods you need to know to be a good investor.

Part 1 helps you master the mental side of investing by revealing the **mindset** shifts it takes to be a successful investor.

Part 2 outlines the **principles** of investing. These will provide the foundation from which you will make all of your investing decisions.

In **Part 3**, we'll combine the investing mindset you have developed and principles you have learned to create **methods** you can use to invest in different scenarios.

Finally, this book has three appendices. The first explains how to select a financial advisor, what to expect when you work with one and how to get the most out of your relationship with your financial advisor. The second is a list of the questions people frequently ask about investing. The third is a brief list of guidelines to remember as you invest.

After you have read this book, you will have the necessary knowledge and confidence to take control of your future financial security. Life is richer when you make good financial decisions, and not just in terms of wealth. Financial security leads to peace of mind—and the chance to live your life to the fullest.

PART I

MINDSET

The hardest, most important part of investing is developing the necessary mindset to take the right actions. This portion of the book will explore six mental paradigm shifts you need to experience in order to make sound investment decisions.

1. **Simplicity vs. Complexity**: Complex investments may *seem* better, but a simple approach may yield better long-term outcomes.

2. **Investing vs. Speculating**: Moving in and out of risky investments is fun, but investing is the better way to grow your wealth in the long-term.

3. **Wisdom vs. Information**: It is easy to get caught up in the neverending stock-market-news cycle. Investors who can tune it out and rely on timeless wisdom instead make better investing decisions.

4. **Long-term vs. Short-term:** The formula for success requires finding the right solution to the right problem for the right time frame.

5. **Processes vs. Goals:** Developing and executing a process is more important than setting goals.

6. **Delusion vs. Reality:** Focus on what you can control and stop worrying about the things beyond your control.

CHAPTER 1

SIMPLICITY VS. COMPLEXITY

"Simplicity is the ultimate sophistication."

—Leonardo da Vinci

I n the mid-1300s, a philosopher named William of Ockham created a principle to help him make decisions. It became known as *Occam's Razor* and it "shaves" away undesirable choices, making decisions easier.

The principle states that among competing hypotheses leading to the same outcome, the one which is the simplest should be selected.

Always selecting the simplest choice seems like common sense. If you had to choose between two paths which both arrive at the same place, why would you choose one that is longer, riskier or more expensive to take?

You wouldn't, of course. Yet investors choose complexity over simplicity all the time.

Some complexity is inevitable, especially as the size of your portfolio grows. It is a natural byproduct of financial success. Complexity which does not yield an advantage, however, is always bad.

Here are a few examples of complexity that often creep into investment portfolios, inhibiting their performances.

- Rather than owning all of their mutual funds in one brokerage account, an investor will have many accounts open, with various mutual-fund holdings in each.

- Rather than having a simple portfolio diversification method, an investor will set up a complex scheme for which instruments they should use and which sectors of the market into which they should buy.

- Rather than buying a simple mutual fund or ETF, an investor will build and maintain a personal stock portfolio.

- Rather than rolling over all of their accounts into a single account, an investor will have multiple employer-sponsored retirement accounts, such as a 401(k) and a 403(b).

- Rather than using a financial product such as an ETF, an investor will use complex financial products such as stock options, derivatives or other structured products.

The Price of Complexity

In each of the examples above, the investor is trying to achieve a better return by adding complexity to their portfolios. Or perhaps they are not engaged enough with their investments to remove unnecessary complexity. Either way, failing to accurately account for the effects of complexity can lead to the long-term erosion of their wealth.

Complex investment strategies usually require more maintenance and entail higher overhead costs. At investment firms, they require more people and technology to run and the associated fees get passed on to the investors. For private investors, complexity costs additional time and energy to learn and maintain.

Inevitably, complexity inhibits strategic clarity. When you have too many elements in your portfolio—even if it is just several different retirement accounts—you will begin to lose sight of the overall picture. When that happens, you begin to miss out on opportunities to optimize your investment portfolio.

With your strategy blurred, it becomes easy to make mistakes. More accounts and more moving parts within those accounts increases the chances that investments will go awry.

When you find your wealth management veering towards complexity, know you are not maximizing your potential return. Whether through additional overhead, a murky strategy or small mistakes, complexity can cost you.

Once you realize where you have allowed complexity to creep in, follow these five steps to regain simplicity in your investments.

1. **Consolidate Accounts**. Having too many accounts makes it difficult to keep track of your overall strategy. With time, it becomes harder to keep track of how any one account should be invested or how it relates to the others. Maintain as few accounts as necessary.

2. **Eliminate Redundancy**. Think of your portfolio like a fine-tuned watch with precisely the right number and type of springs, screws and gears. Every investment you own should perform a different, useful function. If any are not, eliminate them.

3. **Reduce Quantity**. Consolidate individual investments where possible. Rather than owning a high number of stocks you may want to consider a mutual fund that can achieve approximately the same outcome via a simpler instrument.

4. **Forgo Customization**. Instead of designing your own investment instruments, save yourself time and money by using *off-the-shelf* solutions.

5. **Be Wary of Unconventional Investments**. Your advisor should be able to explain any investment program in less than five minutes. If it takes longer than that, or if you have heard the presentation and you still do not fully understand it, be cautious.

Once you have regained simplicity in your portfolio, keep it simple. Develop a philosophy of pursuing simplicity wherever possible in your finances.

The strategy with the least complexity which achieves a desired result is usually the best, most profitable choice. Take *Occam's Razor* with you and shave off unnecessary complexity every chance you get.

CHAPTER 2

INVESTING VS. SPECULATING

"Speculation becomes dangerous the minute you begin to take it seriously."

—Benjamin Graham

Two types of people put money into the market: investors and speculators. Because both types of traders are pursuing a return on their money, they are often mistaken for each other. They are, however, very different, and their respective styles yield wildly different results.

Investors use a defined strategy, holding a diversified portfolio for an appropriate amount of time depending on their goals. Speculators use reckless abandon, moving into and out of positions often, always chasing a quick buck.

Investors usually win in the long run by making steady gains off of the growth and rising profits of the businesses in which they are invested. Speculators usually eventually lose their money to trading fees and excessive risk.

Speculation

The word speculator comes from the Latin *specere*, meaning to *spy* or *look out*. Speculators are constantly looking for tips, rumors or news on which to base their decisions. A speculator might hear that a company will have a better than expected earnings report and then buy the stock to try to make an overnight profit.

Speculators share many traits with gamblers, whose decisions are also based on hunches or gut feelings. A speculator may feel a certain stock is about to fall and short the stock in order to take advantage of the drop.

As with gambling, chance makes a quick profit possible. Also like gambling, the trader will usually lose to the "house" in the long run. When that happens, a speculator is likely to continue feeding money into his account, hoping to try his luck at striking it big just one more time.

Because it often yields poor long-term results, in my opinion, speculation has no place in serious investment plans. If you are not sure if you are speculating, read the following five statements. If any of them describe your actions, then you may be speculating.

1. You are focused on short-term results.

2. You are not diversifying.

3. You are actively trading stock options.

4. You are day-trading.

5. You are trading based on recent news reports.

Of course, speculating can be fun in the same way going to a casino can be fun. So human nature compels some people to speculate, even though they know it is not the best use of their money. If you do speculate, follow these guidelines:

- Realize you are speculating, not investing.

- Speculate with no more than 10% of your portfolio.

- Conduct your speculations in a dedicated account.

- Only trade what you can afford to lose.

- Never increase your initial speculation deposit.

Additionally, do not expect your financial advisor to give you advice on your speculation efforts. Excellent financial advisors are not speculators. They diligently find ways to achieve the best return on investments; speculation is rarely one of those ways.

Investing

In contrast to the wild swings of speculation, investing comes with the expectation of slow, steady gains. Investors expect a return on their money over a predetermined time frame which matches their investing goals.

Investing does not try to extract value from the market through wild trades like speculation does. Instead, it allows investors to harness the wealth-building potential of the stock market, and in turn, the economic engines of the United States and other countries. Investing drives companies and countries forward often providing a return for the investor.

Finally, investing in stocks lets you become an owner of a business by giving you actual equity. Very few people become wealthy because of their paycheck, no matter how much they earn. Wealth is usually generated through equity—owning investments such as stock or privately-held businesses.

Successful investing is rarely achieved by weaving recklessly in and out of stocks. It is achieved by building a portfolio that takes into consideration an investor's risk tolerance, experience and goals and then adjusting the portfolio only slightly over time as necessary. In my experience, that is the best way to create wealth and achieve long-term financial security.

CHAPTER 3

INFORMATION VS. WISDOM

Absorb what is useful.
Discard what is useless.

—Bruce Lee

E very day, the financial news media, the internet, friends, family, your colleagues and your Uber driver spew a cacophony of information at you—stock market updates, hot stock tips, geopolitical developments and financial news flashes. If you listen to them and act on the information, you will quickly fall into frenetic speculation.

The easiest way to identify what is merely "information" is by its shelf life. The value of information, if there is any at all, expires rapidly. Using it as your guide for investing is like navigating by a star that is constantly changing its position in the sky. Information which is only pertinent for the next few hours should have no impact on your 20-year investment strategy.

While taking in this information seems innocuous, it will detrimentally affect your trading. You will become a slave to the whims of those around you, rather than enjoying the freedom of investing based on sound principles and a concrete strategy. Imbibing a steady stream of financial information usually leads to financial problems.

The Problems with Information Intake

Problem 1: You will base your actions on the histrionics of financial "news" sources. The stock market media creates a steady supply of fresh, tantalizing information, but their interests are misaligned with yours. They are in the business of selling ads, not financial advice, and they will say whatever it takes to get you to watch the next commercial break or click to the next page of the article.

Problem 2: You will begin trading based on price movements. If you see prices are down, you become upset; afraid to incur any more losses, you decide to sell. If you hear prices are up, you get excited; in the hopes that they will continue to go up, you buy. You sell low and buy high—the exact opposite of good investing.

Problem 3: You will check your investments more frequently. As you consume the steady stream of financial information, you will be compelled to keep checking your investments to see what new news has come out.

The more you check your investments, the more likely you are to make changes that hurt your long-term performance.[1] Investors who check their investments too often end up overestimating the amount of risk they are taking. They decrease their risk profile, preventing themselves from making a sufficient return to meet their goals.

In other words, when you see the performance of your investments too often, you will *react to your perception* of the market instead of *responding to the reality* of the market. Perceptive reactions are emotional and often inaccurate. They prevent profit or lead to a long-term loss. Reality-based responses are strategic and realistic. They often lead to long-term gains.

Cutting Back on Information

To be a successful investor, you need to learn how to tune out information. It serves no useful purpose in your investing. Here are four ways to go on an information diet:

1. Stop watching financial entertainment shows such as CNBC, Bloomberg and Mad Money.

2. Do not listen to financial radio shows or podcasts on your commute.

3. Unsubscribe from newsletters which peddle stock tips of the day.

---

1   Thaler, R. H., A. Tversky, D. Kahneman, and A. Schwartz. "The Effect of Myopia and Loss Aversion on Risk Taking: An Experimental Test." *The Quarterly Journal of Economics* 112, no. 2 (1997): 647-61. doi:10.1162/003355397555226.

4. Stop using portfolio tracker apps that give you up-to-the-minute stock quotes on your smartphone or computer.

The Benefits of Wisdom

Once you have removed useless information from your life, you will need to fill the void with something profitable. Fortunately, there is something to which you can pay attention that will help you respond, rather than react. It is a word you do not hear much anymore, especially as applied to investing: *wisdom*. My favorite definition of *wisdom* is that it is the accumulation of human knowledge that can be applied to solve a problem.

Whereas information expires quickly, wisdom is timeless. It is as useful today as it was 50 years ago, and it will be just as useful 50 years from now. Because wisdom does not change over time, it gives you a strong foundation from which to invest.

For example, The Intelligent Investor by Benjamin Graham was first published in 1949. Its content is still relevant today. Likewise, the majority of this book is accumulated investment wisdom which will always be helpful for investing.

Here are a few examples of the wisdom covered in more detail in upcoming chapters:

- The benefits of having a long-term plan (see Chapter 4).

- The progress which comes from using processes instead of goals (see Chapter 5).

- The futility of trying to predict the future (see Chapter 8).

- The importance of diversification (see Chapter 12).

As you can see, wisdom is also broadly applicable—these are universal principles of success that are simply being applied here to investing. While information is specific to a single stock or trade, the wisdom learned here can be used in many areas of your life.

Learn to turn a deaf ear to useless, trivial information. Instead, seek out wisdom, learn it inside and out, and use it as the foundation for your investment philosophy. Instead of experiencing the severe side effects of consuming information, you will experience the financial health that accompanies wisdom.

CHAPTER 4

LONG-TERM VS. SHORT-TERM

Someone is sitting in the shade today because someone planted a tree a long time ago.

—Warren Buffett

Imagine if the government devised a solution to poverty. Every man, woman and child would receive an annual check for $50,000. If everything went as planned, homelessness and hunger would be stamped out overnight.

However, other problems would immediately crop up. People would start having more children to get more checks. Others who were gainfully employed would stop working, causing economic growth to slow. Tax revenues would decrease and social programs would have to be cut. Long-term problems—in this case, poverty—always require long-term solutions, and short-term problems require short-term solutions.

Often, it's tempting to mismatch the type of problem with the type of solution. The appeal of short-term financial solutions like Certificates of Deposit is that they offer relative safety compared to long-term solutions. Safety is important, but if you have a long-term objective, then the safety of a short-term solution is a trap. Playing it safe will cause you to miss out on the opportunity to generate significant wealth.

On the other hand, the appeal of long-term solutions like investing in the stock market is that they can produce higher rates of return. It is easy to overlook, though, that they may experience short-term declines. If you are saving for a short-term goal and pick an investment with a higher rate of return, you will not have enough time to reap the full return and may be stuck in the investment in the event of a downturn.

Here are four investing scenarios in which investors fail to match the time frame of the problem with the time frame of the solution.

- **Saving for a house**—Someone planning to purchase a house in the next few years wants to earn a return on their money while they are saving up, so they decide to invest in a startup. When it's time to purchase their house, they are unable to liquidate their investment.

- **Investing extra cash**—A nonprofit receives a generous donation, and the board of directors wants to earn interest on it until they decide what to do with it. They decide to invest it in the stock market. The market drops precipitously, and they are left waiting for it to recover until they can use the donation.

- **Retirement savings**—Someone saving for retirement puts all of their money into CDs. When they reach retirement, they find out their savings goal will not be met until they are 150.

- **College savings**—A future college student decides to save for college with a savings account. They may eventually save enough for college, but they would have a much higher return on their investment if they used a long-term solution for their long-term problem.

When you are determining how to invest, avoid the impulse to choose the solution with the highest return or the greatest safety. Take a step back and analyze whether you are investing for the short-term or the long-term; then, choose your solution accordingly.

By avoiding mismatching the problem and the solution, you achieve the optimum balance between growing your money and making sure it is accessible when you need it.

CHAPTER 5

GOALS VS. PROCESSES

You do not rise to the level of your goals. You fall to the level of your systems.

—James Clear

You might think hyper-successful people like Olympic athletes or Fortune 500 executives are obsessively focused on their goals. Yet many of the top performers in their field are quick to credit their success to their use of processes.

"If you're really focusing on the outcome and just winning, then you can become fearful. But, if you just focus on the process, the process is fearless."—Joe Madden, 2015 Baseball World Series winning coach

> *"I... focus on my process. [I] don't care about the result."*—Rory McIlroy, PGA golfer

> *"Concentrate on what will produce results rather than on the results, the process rather than the prize."*—Bill Walsh, three-time Super Bowl Champion and two-time NFL Coach of the Year

> *"Thinking about winning can pull your focus off of proper execution in a competition. Thinking about process is the answer."*—Lanny Bassham, Olympic Gold Medalist and performance coach

Investors have the same options as professional athletes and coaches. They can choose to focus on goals, such as having a net worth of $2 million by the time they retire. Or they can focus on processes, such as setting aside $1,500 every month for retirement.

Both the goal-setter and the process-follower have the same achievement in mind: the financial means to accomplish some purpose. But like their sports counterparts, the process-follower investor is far more likely to be successful. Why?

Simply, goals do not work well with human nature. While goals provide a concrete destination, they do not tell you how to get there. Imagine climbing into your car for a new road trip without a map or GPS. You may have a fun ride, but the chances of getting to your intended destination are rather low.

Goals also bring additional stress into your investment planning, causing you to constantly worry about failing to meet them. If your portfolio falls, you will be tempted to make unwise decisions—such as speculating—in order to bring it back in line with your goals.

Goals are easy to bend—surely it's okay if you use some of that retirement account now, as long as you put it back later. Finally, goals can be procrastinated on until it is too late to make up for the procrastination.

Processes eliminate all of goals' shortcomings. They provide clear, easy-to-follow directions for how you should get from where you are to where you want to be. Your job is to just get behind the steering wheel and drive.

They relieve you of the stress of having to make decisions. All you have to do is make the deposit into the account. If the market drops, you just keep making deposits. Because your process does not include withdrawals, you never make any.

Because processes are automatic, they are harder to procrastinate on. Once you get into the rhythm of investing, or automate your portfolio entirely, you will have to work against momentum in order to put off making deposits into your retirement account.

Using processes gives investors an immense advantage over those who do not. While other investors are investing erratically to meet their goals, you will be calmly investing with consistent, repeatable processes.

To identify the processes you should follow, you must isolate the things which lead to the result you want. The good news is other people have already discovered which processes are likely to work and which are not. A good financial advisor can help you determine the specific processes which will help you meet your goals.

Once you have identified the processes, you no longer need to pay attention to the short-term performance of your investments. You only need to focus on continually executing only your processes. If you do, you are likely to be successful. Good investment outcomes are the result of good investing processes.

CHAPTER 6

DELUSION VS. REALITY

"Freedom is... won by disregarding things that lie beyond our control."

–Epictetus

Very few things in investing can be directly controlled. People still assume, however, consciously or subconsciously, that they can exert control over:

- The stock market's movements
- The U.S. economy
- The interest rate
- The news media

But attempting to directly control any of these things is futile. A key to successful investing is discerning which things you can and cannot control and allocating your time and energy accordingly. The moment you do so is the moment you gain control over your financial future.

You can develop your own strategy. Set goals, define your risk profile, choose your investments, delineate a timeframe, allocate your funds, review and rebalance your portfolio, and monitor it over time to ensure your strategy is working (for more on this, see Chapter 13).

You can set your own expectations for your strategy. Every investor has a set of expectations as to how their investments will perform. Set realistic expectations; when investments go down, you will calmly hold and wait for your strategy to play out.

You can control your own behavior as you execute your strategy. Your behavior is either your greatest asset or your greatest liability. Bring it under your own control so when an investment decision needs to be made, you can respond rather than react (for more on behavior in investing, see Chapter 7).

You can decide your own costs. Investment returns are always variable, but investment expenses are usually fixed. Avoid financial instruments with high expenses and keep frequent trades to a minimum.

You can choose your own advisors. As your savings grow, it becomes more advantageous to work with a financial advisor. Find and use a good financial advisor who can help you create a master plan for your money, so that you know where you are going and can make sure you will get there.

You can affect your taxes. You cannot control tax policy, but you can affect the amount of taxes you pay by using tax-efficient investment strategies. The IRS is your silent partner—if you receive capital gains, dividends, or any type of financial gain, they will get their cut. Minimize their take by using tax-advantaged accounts and investments.

The important thing to remember is most of what happens is beyond your control. When you focus on what you can control, you become powerful and you make better decisions. It takes time and discipline to cultivate this mindset, but it leads to superior results.

PART II

PRINCIPLES

"As to methods there may be a million and then some, but principles are few. The man who grasps principles can successfully select his own methods. The man who tries methods, ignoring principles, is sure to have trouble."

—Ralph Waldo Emerson

Many people run into trouble while investing because they focus on methods first, ignoring principles. They think they can find the perfect method with which to invest. But there is no magic formula for investing success. Successful investors' secrets lie not in the methods they use, but in the principles to which they adhere.

This is a set of seven important investing principles. The first three are forces which work against you, the second three are forces which work for you, and the last shows you how to combine the forces into a successful investment strategy.

CHAPTER 7

BIASES INHIBIT GOOD DECISIONS

A bias recognized is a bias sterilized.

–Benjamin Haydon

A Vanguard study found a good financial advisor can add 1.5% to a client's net returns solely through behavioral coaching.[2] Over the course of a $1,000,000, 40-year investment, that would yield an additional $800,000. Why does having someone who can help investors learn how their brain thinks have such an outsized effect on investment performance?

---

2 "Quantifying Your Value to Your Clients." Vanguard Advisor's Alpha. Accessed February 05, 2018. https://advisors. vanguard.com/iwe/pdf/FASQAAAB.pdf.

The answer is simple. Crisis management is governed by the limbic system, which is the brain's self-protective mechanism. It determines whether you fight, run or freeze in the face of an attack. When making this decision, the brain naturally chooses to use its quicker reflex, emotion, over its slower reflex, reason.

Unfortunately, the emotional state of mind is not the ideal state in which to make decisions. It can easily be triggered by a false alarm, such as when the Dow Jones suddenly dips 1,000 points. Your mind immediately goes into survival mode and you close all of your positions as fast as possible.

Later, your rational mind kicks in. You remember the long-term performance of the market is always superior to the prevention of short-term losses. But it's too late— the market has recovered, but your shrunken portfolio has not.

Here are several of the most common ways your mind can detrimentally affect how you invest.

Pattern Recognition. Over millions of years, our species has developed a keen ability to recognize patterns. Humans who were good at spotting prey and predators and distinguishing poisonous plans from edible ones survived, passing on their pattern recognition genes.

Now, you are a finely tuned pattern-recognition machine. If an event occurs three times in a row, your brain automatically anticipates that it will happen again. Sometimes, your brain will work so hard to see a pattern that it will imagine one where one does not even exist.

The problem is that pattern recognition does not work in investing. Past performance never predicts future performance—and if it did, someone would already have exploited it.

Confirmation Bias. By default, your brain looks for information to support its own views. When the brain is analyzing data, it will focus on that which supports its own views and ignore or reinterpret that which does not.

This can be powerfully observed in people who try to game the market. They will develop a theory, then look at only the historical data which supports the theory in order to prove that it works.

Loss Aversion. People feel the pain of losing more strongly than the enjoyment of winning. Research shows that most people feel the impact of a loss twice as strongly as they feel a gain of the same size.

Investors who fall prey to the psychology of loss aversion adopt a low risk profile to keep from losing money. They will not, however, end up making much money from their investments, either.

Follower Bias. People want to do the things that other people are doing. That is part of the reason Bitcoin soared at the end of 2017. By the time there is a crowd to follow, though, the gains are usually nearly gone—leaving you holding a sinking investment.

Excessive Optimism or Pessimism. Some investors believe the market will perpetually rise. Others think the next crash is just around the corner. The former will put too much money in the market, while the latter will keep too much money under their pillows. Neither will do as well as the investor who understands the risks associated with the market and invests accordingly.

Overconfidence. If you overestimate your ability in a given situation, failing to validate or test your ideas before committing to an investment, you will most likely lose money.

Illusion of Control. Some investors, consciously or subconsciously, think they can control the movement of the stock market. They cannot.

Fear of Missing Out. In rising markets, investors begin to fear that if they do not invest all of their money, they will miss out on the gains. Even the most conservative investors will pour their money into the stock market after they hear how much their friends have recently made. When the market inevitably falls, they lose even more money than their friends.

Heuristics. Heuristics are mental shortcuts for investing. You have probably heard a few: You should retire and take Social Security at age 62. A 4% IRA withdrawal rate is good. Bonds are always safe. Heuristics can be good, but they should not be used to make major decisions. Each of the decisions mentioned above should be tailored to your specific financial situation.

All of these mindsets and biases cause investors to deviate from their strategies and to make poor decisions. In the end, they usually lose money.

Some investors reading this list may believe they already understand and can counteract their internal biases. Often, however, intelligence makes a person even more susceptible to them. Regardless of your investing experience or proclivities, it is easy for you to sabotage your financial future by making emotion-filled snap judgements.

Since your behavioral discipline will play a large role in your investing success, how can you adjust your brain's default settings in order to make better decisions and experience a better investment outcome?

- Know that your mind has specific biases. Self-awareness is a powerful first step towards making better decisions.

- Be aware of the factors which affect your mindset. There is an acronym which helps identify if you are in a bad frame of mind to make an important decision: HALT—Hungry, Angry, Lonely or Tired. If any of those describe you, then you should delay making major decisions until you are in a better frame of mind.

- Remember the two emotions that cause FOG in all investors' minds: Fear Or Greed. If you are basing your decisions on either of these, it will be difficult to make a good decision.

- Use your values as a guide. When all else fails, filter your decisions through your investing values. This can keep you from making impulsive decisions that are unaligned with your goals.

Most investors spend far more time reading about investing than they do about behavior and mindsets. Knowing how to control what you think and feel while investing, however, can have a greater impact on your success than even choosing the right financial instruments.

CHAPTER 8

INFLATION
REDUCES RETURNS

Inflation is as violent as a mugger, as frightening as an armed robber and as deadly as a hit man.

—Ronald Reagan

After your own mind, inflation is one of the biggest threats to your investment efforts. It's like weeds in your garden: If you do not continually invest money at a return that is higher than inflation, then you will end up losing the majority of your capital to it.

For example, if inflation is 2% this year, the purchasing power of each dollar in your account will decline by 2%. If inflation averages 2% annually for the next 10 years, the purchasing power of each dollar in your account will have decreased by 22% at the end of the 10-year period.

Over short periods of time, inflation is relatively harmless. But over a long period of time, it can do serious damage to the value of a portfolio. A $100,000 portfolio in 1988 would be able to buy less than $50,000 worth of investments today, in inflation-adjusted dollars.

While economists have not reached a consensus on what causes inflation, they generally agree that when the economy grows, consumers purchase more goods. Demand outstrips supply, and producers raise prices. Over time, each dollar can purchase fewer goods and services than it could before.

Figure 8.1: The price of goods since 1975 [3]

	1975	**1987**	**2000**	**2018**
Stamp	$0.10	$0.22	$0.33	$0.50
Gasoline	$0.57	$0.90	$1.51	$2.85
Movie Ticket	$2.03	$3.91	$5.39	$8.97
Gallon of Milk	$1.57	$2.28	$2.79	$3.13

---

3   Source for Fig 8.1 and for the next paragraph. Bureau of Labor Statistics. Consumer Price Index Data. Accessed March 27, 2019. www.bls.gov/cpi/

Annual inflation has averaged about 3% since 1926. In the 1970s, it averaged around 8%, but in the 2010s, it averaged only 1.5%. Economists see inflation between 2-4% as indicative of a healthy economy.

Because the causes of inflation are not well understood, and the annual effects of inflation are so small, many investors focus only on the preservation or growth of their money. But the growth rate of real dollars and the growth rate of purchasing power are two very different things:

- The growth rate of the dollars in your account is known as the "nominal return."

- The growth rate of the purchasing power of the dollars in your account is known as the "real return."

In other words, real return is the increase of the purchasing power of your money after inflation has been factored in. Imagine that you put your money in a CD paying 2%, and inflation for the year was 3%. The amount of money in your account would have grown by 2% (nominal return), but your purchasing power would have decreased by 1% (real return).

You are investing money for use at some point in the future, which means that it will be affected by inflation. As you plan your investments, you should care about the real return, not the nominal return.

Inflation harms people who want to "play it safe" the most. Consider a couple that retires at age 62. The $1 million they have in their retirement savings accounts represents all the money they have for retirement. Once it's gone, it's gone.

They know that they will not have time to recover from a big market loss, so they want to invest in something that is not as risky: CDs. During the early years of their retirement, things appear okay. Income sources such as Social Security, CD interest and pensions allow them to maintain a healthy lifestyle.

Over the next 18 years, inflation averages 3.1%; interest on their CD is only 1%. In their early eighties, when they begin to need more money for health care, the purchasing power of their retirement savings has dropped by nearly 50%. In real terms, a $10,000 medical bill will now cost $14,500. Their initial $1 million retirement savings has effectively been reduced to $687,000—all while they were attempting to preserve their capital.

To protect your money from inflation, you must invest in assets that offer a higher return than the rate of inflation. Otherwise, you will eventually find that the cost of everything has doubled—and your assets have not. Safely and slowly, you will go broke.

CHAPTER 9

THE MARKET IS UNBEATABLE

Investments work; investors don't.

—Unknown

O
ne of the mental biases outlined in Chapter 7 was overconfidence. The natural end product of overconfidence is the false conclusion that, given enough time and research, the market can be beat.

To that end, investors create new, complex investment models using sophisticated technology and technical terminology. Their shiny creations rarely work in the long term. More often than not, they mete out a costly punishment to their inventors.

By studying how other investors have failed, you can keep yourself from the illusion of market control. Here are four major approaches private investors often use to try to beat the market.

Gut Feeling

Many investors mistakenly believe that they or someone they know can devise a way to accurately forecast the stock market's short-term performance. But there is no evidence of anyone accurately doing so over an extended period of time. There is, however, a preponderance of empirical evidence showing that the stock market's movements cannot be accurately predicted.

Barron's, a reputable business publication, prints Barron's Roundtable, a list of stock market predictions for the upcoming year from investment professionals on Wall Street. Year after year, it provides evidence that even the top professionals on Wall Street are clueless as to what the stock market is going to do in the short run.

The 2008 Roundtable report was titled "A Bullish Call—Wall Street's seers forecast gains for stocks next year." All 12 experts on the panel forecasted that the stock market would have a positive return, with predictions varying from a high of 18% to a low of 3%. In reality, 2008 was the worst year for the stock market since 1930—the Dow lost 37%.

Not only do the most well-financed, well-educated, well-equipped, experienced investors fail to predict bear markets, but they also do not see bull markets coming. In 2017, an article in Barron's predicted a 7% return; the actual return was more than 19%. [4]

---

4   Barron's, Outlook 2017, This Bull Market Has Legs, December 17, 2016

Here's another example. In 1959, Alan Greenspan told Fortune Magazine that stocks were overvalued.[5] The market went up 43% the next year. In an interview in 1973, he urged investors to buy stocks without hesitation: "It's very rare that you can be as unqualifiedly bullish as you can now." [6] Within 16 months of that statement, the Dow Jones had dropped 50% and the economy plummeted to depths unseen since the Great Depression.

Alan had a bachelor's, master's and PhD degree in economics, and he would later hold the position of Chairman of the Federal Reserve for two decades. If neither he nor any other eminent investor or institution can predict the market's future accurately, you and I do not stand a chance.

Technical or Quantitative Analysis

Chapter 7 also outlined the bias of pattern recognition. Technical investors try to predict future stock market performance by identifying patterns in past market data. These patterns will purportedly tip them off to future price movements. They are not concerned with the actual investments or underlying fundamentals—only the shapes they see in the charts.

They have names for the shapes they see. Even the names are ridiculous, which makes it surprising that many "professional" investors pay attention to them.

---

5   Fortune Magazine, March Issue, 1959

6   New York Times, January 7, 1973

Here are a few good ones:

- Dead cat bounce

- Candlestick

- Cup and handle

- Head and shoulders top

- Double top and bottom

- Triple top and triple bottom

You do not want to make investment decisions based on imaginary shapes you can see in the charts, any more than you want to make major life decisions based on the pattern tea leaves make at the bottom of a tea cup.

Formula Investing

Formula investing uses a predetermined set of rules, like a computer program, to determine in advance how investments will be managed.

For example, the Motley Fool promoted a formula investing technique called "The Foolish Four." They wrote a book titled "The Foolish Four: How to Crush Your Mutual Funds in 15 Minutes a Year."

This was their formula...

1. Take the five stocks in the Dow Jones with the lowest stock prices and highest dividend yields.

2. Discard the one with the lowest price.

3. Put 40% of your money in the stock with the second-lowest price.

4. Put 20% in each of the three remaining stocks.

5. One year later, sort the Dow the same way and reset the portfolio according to steps 1 through 4.

6. Repeat until rich.

You're probably wondering how the Foolish Four formula worked. Let's just say the Motley Fool is no longer promoting this approach. Their website now says, "Mechanical investing can be a very risky and highly volatile way to invest and many things can go wrong. Not every strategy works out, and even those that look very promising may crash." We'll take their word for it.

Indicator Investing

Indicator investing uses specific, market-wide movements to predict future market performance. For example, the First Five Days of January indicator proposes that if the market has a positive return for the first five days of the year, then it will have a positive return for the full year.

There are just two problems. The indicator only works if the market's return over that time frame is positive. If it is negative, the results are about 50/50. And if you extend the return time frame back to when the Dow Jones first opened, you will be far better off just keeping your money in the market the entire time.

The next time you hear a financial "expert" on TV or read a mailer from a "guru" predicting what the stock market is going to do next year, just remind yourself no human is capable of that feat—and if they were, they certainly would not tell you.

If you ever feel the urge to predict the market yourself, do not invest real money. Instead, write down your prediction, stick it in an envelope, and date it. Then, see how it turns out over time.

CHAPTER 10

THE MARKET RISES OVER TIME

"The average long-term experience in investing is never surprising."

—Charles Ellis

According to a study by Vanguard, if you invest in the stock market and take your money out after one year, you have a one in four chance of losing money. If you invest for 10 years and then take your money out, you have a one in 25 chance of losing money. After 20 years, zero.[7]

That's because in the short term, the stock market is volatile and unpredictable. However, over longer

---

7   "How Risk, Reward & Time Are Related." Vanguard. Accessed February 04, 2019. https://investor.vanguard.com/investing/how-to-invest/risk-reward-compounding.

periods of time, the performance of the stock market is remarkably consistent. In the face of short-term uncertainty, profitability comes from long-term consistency.

To take advantage of the consistently positive long-term returns of the stock market, you need to give your investments the time they need. If a cake recipe says to bake it for 20 minutes, but you decide to take it out of the oven after 10, your cake will be about half the size it should be and will have an awful texture. If you do not give your investments the time they need to produce results, you will end up with a portfolio half the size it should be and it will be in awful shape.

Remember: Over long periods of time, the stock market has consistently produced a positive return. Whereas in the short-term, stock market declines are normal. So let time work for you by investing for the long-term.

Your investment goals are almost never short-term. You don't expect to withdraw the money in a month or a year. Your goals (college, retirement, etc.) are long-term goals. Because your goals and objectives are long-term, you should focus on the long-term ability of investments to produce the type of returns they historically have.

CHAPTER 11

RISK EQUALS REWARD

The biggest risk is not taking any risk.

—Mark Zuckerberg

"R isk" is one of the most misunderstood words in investing. Understanding what risk means in the context of investing is important because properly leveraged, it can be a powerful force you can use to your advantage.

In investing, risk does not mean the chance of losing your money permanently. It means the fluctuation of your investments as compared to the overall market. The term used to describe those fluctuations is volatility—volatility is a measure of risk. The greater the fluctuation, the greater the volatility.

A savings account carries no volatility, and $1 invested in a savings account will always nominally be worth at least $1. A dollar invested in a stock, though, can rise or fall dramatically. Therefore, stocks are more volatile (risky) than savings accounts.

An investment's level of return is linked with its risk. The higher the risk, the higher the return; the lower the risk, the lower the return. After all, if you are willing to take on risky investments, you should be rewarded for it.

Figure 11.1: Volatility versus average return across asset classes [8]

Asset Class	Volatility	20-Year Avg. Return
Cash	0.59	1.97%
Bonds	3.36	4.98%
Diversified Portfolio	10.56	6.72%
Large Cap Value	14.92	7.39%
Small / Mid Cap Stocks	18.40	9.12%
REITs	19.52	8.67%

---

8   "20 Years of the Best and Worst: A Case for Diversification." MFS. February 04, 2019.

Modern Portfolio Theory

Harry Markowitz was the first person to explain the relationship between risk and return in investing. He theorized that the higher the risk (volatility), the greater the potential return; the lower the risk, the lower the potential return. He won a Nobel Prize for what became known as the "modern portfolio theory."

The theory revealed that for each increment of risk, there is an optimal investment mix which will produce the best return. You can use his theory to make risk work for you by designing your investment mix to optimize risk against return in accordance with your goals.

The theory also teaches that without risk, there is no return—which helps you start to look at risk differently. It is not necessarily bad. It is just something which leads to the returns you want. It does not mean a permanent loss. It just means your investments will swing in value. If you can mentally and financially handle those swings, you should use risk to your advantage.

Occasionally, you will hear about a great investment opportunity with the promise of a high rate of return with little or no risk. This investment violates the principle of risk and return, and it is a scam (unless the person offering it has discovered a new paradigm of thinking about investing, in which case you should nominate them for a Nobel Prize).

The A.R.T. of Risk Management

There are only three ways to face risk: You can avoid it, retain it or transfer it.

You can **avoid** risk by not taking on any. This means your money will not have any volatility, but it also will not grow. One dollar in a savings account may grow slightly with minimal interest and will always be worth at least one dollar. Avoiding risk will bring you peace of mind in the short-term, but it will not lead to wealth creation in the long-term.

You can **retain** risk by taking risk on and managing it yourself. This is taking a calculated risk with a realistic expectation for return. This is exactly how good investing works.

You can **transfer** risk by paying someone else to take the risk on for you. This is what insurance companies do for you. They are professional risk managers. Never expect to offload risk for free. Insurance companies charge in proportion to the risk they are taking on.

There is no return without risk. Risk is not necessarily bad. It just needs to be responsibly taken on and managed in order to achieve the returns you need.

CHAPTER 12

DIVERSIFICATION CAN MITIGATE RISK

The best way to insulate yourself from surprises is to diversify.

—Robert Shiller

I f you choose to retain risk, then diversification is one of your best weapons against loss. Of course, diversification does not guarantee positive returns or protection against short-term losses, but it can help shield your portfolio from sudden drops in an asset class or sector.

Diversification entails creating an investment portfolio with different investments which react differently under different market scenarios. For example, if the stock market is going down, you want investments that rise during a market drop. That way, all of your investments do not go down when there is a bad market.

Part of Chapter 13 examines how to diversify your portfolio. For the most part, investors are good at diversifying their portfolio. However, there are a few ways you can accrue concentration risk, which is the risk of losses which may occur from having too much of your money in just a few investments. Here are two of the most common examples of concentration risk.

Inherited Stock

A common instance of concentration risk is from stock that has been inherited from a family member. When someone inherits stock, they are often inclined to hold it based on an emotional attachment, even if it represents an outsized portion of their portfolio.

Perhaps their father was an executive and gave them stock when he died, and now they do not want to sell it because of the connection to their father. Or they may think that since the stock was good for him that it will be good for them.

By holding the stock and having a concentrated position, they are retaining more risk than they realize. Regardless of their emotional attachment, they are better off liquidating at least a portion of the stock and investing it in several other investments.

Company Stock

Holding stock in your employer's company in your 401(k) gives you the opportunity to share in the financial success of the company, but it comes with the risk. If the stock takes a hit, so does your retirement savings. If the company struggles, you may get laid off and the stock could drop, eliminating both your job and your retirement plan.

A study by the Employee Benefits Research Institute and the Investment Company Institute found that of employees who had the opportunity to invest in company stock within their 401(k), 7% had more than 80% of their money in company stock. Of employees that were in their 60s, almost 15% had more than 50% of their savings in company stock.[9]

To mitigate risk through diversification in your 401(k), you should hold no more than 20% of your total assets in your employer's stock at any time, no matter how confident you are in the company for which you work.

The value of diversification has proven itself time and again. Spread your wealth out by placing money in various investments that react differently under the same market circumstances and avoid the trap of putting all your money in just a few investments.

---

[9] Carter, Erik. "When Should You Exercise Your Employee Stock Options?" Forbes. April 14, 2014. Accessed February 04, 2019. https://www.forbes.com/sites/financialfinesse/2012/03/13/when-should-you-exercise-your-options/#78f9806f1680.

CHAPTER 13

STRATEGY

"Strategy is actually very straightforward. You pick a general direction and implement like hell."

—Jack Welch

I f you were to rank the principles every good investor should understand by order of importance, strategy would be at the top of the list. It contributes more to your investment success than any other principle.

Sometimes the word "strategy" can sound intimidating. It seems important and complex and difficult. Strategy simply means *having* and *executing* a purposeful investment plan of action—a master plan—that will allow you to reach your desired destination.

Creating a strategy is not as difficult as it sounds. Here is an eight step process you can use to both design and execute your investing strategy.

1. **ANALYZE**

Investors often dive into "investing" without clarifying what they are investing for. There is no one-size-fits-all approach to investing. Investing for retirement is different than investing to pay for college which is in turn different than investing to buy your first home.

You will be more successful at achieving your desired objective once you have defined what it is and when you want to achieve it. Before you begin strategizing, determine precisely what you are trying to achieve. Ask yourself, "For what am I investing this money? On what will it be spent? When will it be spent?"

2. **STRATEGIZE**

Design a strategy that will make sure you have the money available at the time and for the reason you need it, as outlined in step 1. Ask yourself, "How much risk am I willing—or do I need—to take in order to have that amount of money? In addition, ask yourself the following questions:

- How comfortable am I with risk in investing?
- What type of risk is required to achieve the level of growth I need?
- What limitations of my objective might restrict me from taking risk (e.g., short-term liquidity)?

The risk profile you choose will fall into one of six levels. Knowing these levels (in order from riskiest to most conservative) is helpful in determining which one is right for meeting your investment objectives:

- *Speculative*: You are willing to lose your entire investment for the chance to earn the largest return possible. The time frame is usually very short—from under a minute to a few months. As discussed earlier in this book, speculative efforts do not belong in your serious investment plans.

- *Aggressive*: You seek a high level of return and you expect large swings in value. The time frame for this risk level should be long-term.

- *Growth*: You seek a high level of return and are willing to accept moderate changes in the value of your portfolio. You have a mid- to long-term time frame.

- *Moderate*: You are willing to take some risk to seek higher returns, but you prefer to reduce the possibility of losing principal or having large swings in the value of your account.

- *Conservative*: You prefer low risk and minimal price changes. You accept potentially lower returns as a consequence.

- *Preservative*: Beating inflation is your primary objective. You seek the safest investments possible, and have minimal expectations for growth.

3. **ALLOCATE**

Allocation is the act of selecting a mix of stocks, bonds, cash and other assets that will be necessary to execute your strategy. Different classes of investments respond to changing markets and economies in different ways. For example, stocks often dive during a recession as investors flee high-risk assets. At the same time, government-issued bonds may increase in value as investors pile into low-risk assets.

Allocation among those classes is like measuring the ingredients for cookie batter. The right mix of stocks, bonds, cash and other assets in the right proportion will determine how much volatility your portfolio will experience and how much its value can increase.

One study showed that over 90% of the variability of portfolio performance is driven by asset allocation. Market timing and security selection, however, contributed less than 5% to variability of returns in that study.[10] The outsized impact that asset allocation has on portfolio performances means that it deserves special attention. It can be helpful to work with a professional who can guide you in this area.

_____

10   Brinson, Gary P., L. Randolph Hood, and Gilbert L. Beebower. "Determinants of Portfolio Performance." *Financial Analysts Journal* 51, no. 1 (1995): 133-38. doi:10.2469/faj.v51.n1.1869.

4. **DIVERSIFY**

After allocating your portfolio, the next step is to diversify within each asset class. This includes selecting the sectors, size (large cap, mid cap, small cap), location (domestic, foreign), and valuation (value vs. growth) for stocks. Bonds have their own categories, such as treasury bonds, corporate bonds, municipal bonds, etc.

These "subclasses" rotate in and out of favor. Small cap technology equities were all the rage in the dotcom boom. Then during the bust, investors turned to the safety of large cap stocks. Every investor would love to be in the best-performing asset class every single year.

But it is impossible to consistently predict which asset class or subclass will have the best performance. Instead, diversify into each of the sub-classes listed above in proportion to your objectives and risk tolerance.

5. **INVEST**

Buy the individual stocks, bonds, mutual funds, exchange-traded funds or other investments to fill out your portfolio according to your strategy.

6. **REVIEW**

Conduct an annual due-diligence review of every investment in your portfolio. Look at each investment carefully and make sure that it is still the best fit for the portfolio.

7. **REBALANCE**

Rebalance your portfolio on a scheduled basis to make sure you are staying within your strategy. Rebalancing keeps your investment portfolio in line with your original strategy. It sometimes requires selling a portion of some investments that have grown in order to buy some that have not performed as well. This is a disciplined way to buy low and sell high. It also keeps your portfolio aligned with your desired risk levels.

8. **MONITOR**

Annually review your goals and objectives and make sure that your overall plan is still in line. This is basically going back to step one of the process and making sure your objectives are still the same. If they are, then your portfolio probably does not need to change much.

Notice that this process does not include making changes based on what is happening in the stock market today or based on your gut feeling. It is based on two principles from this section. The market cannot be beat and the market always rises over time. The only time you make changes is when your goals and objectives as identified in Step One have changed.

Creating and executing an investment strategy is better and easier with the help of a professional. A CFP® professional can help remove the obstacles from you being able to successfully execute this system. They can help keep emotions and biases from derailing the execution of your long-term plan. Your long-term plan is your competitive advantage, and you should do everything you can to maximize it.

Whether you are working on your own or with a financial advisor, the process outlined above can be used to design your investment strategy. After completing these eight steps, you will have a strategic investment portfolio with a comfortable amount of risk and a prudent amount of diversification which is designed to accomplish your precise financial objectives.

PART III

METHODS

Investing should be like watching paint dry or watching grass grow.

—Paul Samuelson

Y ou now know the boring truth of successful investing. Essentially, it comprises:

- Building a portfolio which takes into consideration your risk tolerance, experience, goals and time frame.

- Adjusting the portfolio slightly over time as your goals or needs change.

The final part of this book offers specific examples to help you understand how this broad strategy can be successfully used to help you invest under different circumstances.

Now that you have the proper mindset for investing and have internalized its principles, it is time to learn a few practical methods for investing.

INVESTING FOR COLLEGE

C ollege tuition rates have increased an average of 6% every year since the early 1980s—more than double the rate of inflation. That means children born this year will pay more than three times the current tuition rates during their senior year of college.

A target-date fund which has been optimized for your child's age helps make sure you keep up with the rate of college tuition inflation and prevents you from having to take unnecessarily high risk as they near college. This removes the headache from choosing the right investments and monitoring and rebalancing your portfolio.

If you prefer to design your own strategy, you may do so. Using a growth strategy for younger children may give you a little more opportunity for return in the early years; it will, however, require you to manually adjust the portfolio as they get closer to entering college.

The best account to use for college savings is a 529 plan. Each state has its own 529 plan. These accounts are tax-advantaged, meaning that interest grows tax-deferred and is tax-free if used for qualified expenses. You may also get a small tax deduction at the state level if you use a 529, depending on your state.

You can deposit up to $15,000 per year into a 529 plan as an individual or $30,000 as a married couple. You can do a 529 on your own, often with lower expenses, or you can work with a financial advisor.

Coverdell Education Savings Accounts can also help you save for your child's education. CES accounts are limited in their benefit, however. They have low contribution limits, and are not tax deductible.

Even though you should start saving as early as possible, college savings should be secondary to your retirement savings. You and your children can borrow money to pay for college, but you cannot borrow money for your retirement. Once you are saving enough for retirement, you can start setting aside what you can for college.

Do not feel as if you need to save enough to pay for your child's entire college tuition with savings. Many parents who have been successful in covering college costs have used savings as a complement to other methods of paying for school, such as grants, scholarships, and current income.

CHAPTER 15

INVESTING FOR A NONPROFIT

M any nonprofits have excess reserves which they want to invest in order to earn a return. But because of the way nonprofits operate, this can be a very tricky challenge. For example, nonprofits often have boards that rotate frequently, which means a plan one board puts together may not be understood or appreciated by the next board.

In addition, the level of investment experience varies widely on nonprofit boards. Well-meaning board members who are very talented in operations and dedicated to serving the community can make terrible investment choices because they do not have proper experience.

To help solve these challenges, the board should select a committee that is responsible for investing and monitoring the investments. Each member of the committee should have investment knowledge and experience. Many CFP® professionals would gladly serve as pro bono financial consultants or as board members.

Prior to commencing investing, the committee should create an Investment Policy Statement. An IPS details the purpose of the nonprofit's investment account as well as how the committee will go about investing. There are many IPS templates available online for free.

Accounts without specific objectives are difficult to invest for because they lack direction and purpose. An approach that helps to give context to an investment strategy for nonprofits is to earmark certain amounts of money for certain projects or timeframes. This lets the current and future boards know the money in a specific account is for a specific project. Then, you can design the best investment approach for that need.

The board may consider using socially responsible investing, which takes into account both financial return and the way in which the business operates. Socially responsible investing generally eliminates investments in the stock of companies that produce things such as guns, alcohol, tobacco, pornography, etc.

Regardless of the route the board and committee choose, there is always a potential for miscommunication. Staggered board terms can help to minimize gaps in communication, ensuring the nonprofit can maximize the use of its funds. Alternatively, instead of making these decisions themselves, the committee may decide to hire a financial advisor to manage the money.

CHAPTER 16

INVESTING FOR SPECULATION

The title of this chapter is a deliberate misnomer: There is no such thing as investing for speculation. Investing and speculating are two completely different concepts (see Chapter 2).

Speculation is not inherently bad. However, it is like playing with fire. Knowing the properties of fire—it gets hot!—and having the proper safeguards in place will help prevent you from getting burnt.

It is smart to always keep your speculation money in a separate account and to not refill that account. Quarantining your speculating from your investing will help keep the speculation bug from infecting your real investments.

Limit your speculation money to 10% of your investments or the maximum you are willing to lose. That way, if you do lose it, your financial security will not suffer.

And if you win big, you will be that much further ahead of your goals.

Have an exit strategy for your speculative efforts. If you buy a stock at a certain price, know exactly at what point you will sell it. That way, you can at least add a process to your speculation.

Have fun. Speculation in its purest form is gambling, so treat it like a trip to the casino. Enjoy the ride; but again, if you lose big, do not add any more funds to the pot. Take it as a challenge to win it back with your remaining money.

Finally, do not ask your financial advisor about your speculation. In my opinion, if they are a good advisor, they will not want to give you advice about short-term, reactive investing. You want a financial advisor—and the majority of your portfolio—invested in funds which have a strategic, long-term focus.

CHAPTER 17

INVESTING FOR RETIREMENT

The most important thing to do when investing for retirement is to make sure that you are saving enough. Without enough money going into your account through your regular savings, it will not matter how well you invest. A good baseline goal of retirement savings is to aim for 10% of your income, not including any matches your employer will make on your behalf. That percentage will help you accumulate a healthy balance in your retirement account.

Next, make sure your plan addresses the two biggest risks of saving for retirement. The first is inflation. Your investment gains *must* exceed the pace of inflation. The second is self-control. You *must* keep yourself from making the mistake of selling your investments in a bear market.

You can design your own custom portfolio by yourself or you can work with a financial advisor. If you are more than a decade away from retirement, then the best investment strategy will likely be to invest for growth. This calls for a mix that is 80% stocks and 20% bonds. This mix has shown the ability to produce returns that will exceed inflation and grow your purchasing power without unnecessary risk. If you are risk-averse by nature, you might consider a more moderate portfolio. Anything less aggressive than that will not likely grow your assets at the needed pace.

When investing for growth, you should expect that your account balances will fluctuate frequently—often by a lot. This is simply a part of investing. If there were not any risk (volatility), there would not be any returns.

As you near retirement, it will benefit you to meet with a financial advisor skilled in retirement income planning. They can help you re-evaluate your strategy as you start preparing your transition to retirement.

They may walk you through strategies such as adjusting the risk level of your investments to ensure you can withdraw funds as needed, or adjusting to a time-segmented investing strategy to help you prepare for the transition to retirement in time.

CHAPTER 18

INVESTING WHILE RETIRED

S aving for retirement is like spending your lifetime climbing a single mountain. Many financial professionals are proficient at getting you to the top of the financial mountain, ensuring you have enough money to retire when the time comes.

But the most hazardous part of a climb is not the journey to the top of the mountain. It's coming down the mountain that will kill you. Likewise, the most dangerous time period for your investments is during your transition into retirement.

If your footing slips for even a second, you will not have time to recover. Your focus must unerringly shift from growing your money to determining how much retirement income your accumulated resources will produce and the best way to protect that income to ensure financial security.

Six Retirement Risks

As you head into retirement, your income streams face six big obstacles: sequence of returns risk, longevity, inflation, asset/product allocation, excess withdrawal and healthcare. It takes a special financial Sherpa to help you overcome these obstacles and get you down the mountain safely.

- **Sequence of Returns Risk:** This is the risk of not aligning your investment risk with when you will need funds in retirement. For example, if you retire and the market performs poorly in the decade after you retire, it could prevent you from having the funds you need for the rest of retirement.

- **Longevity Risk:** This is the risk of running out of funds before the end of your retirement. Your goal is to set up your investments so they will last for the duration of your retirement.

- **Inflation Risk:** This is purchasing-power risk. While it may seem as if your investment income will be enough for the duration of your retirement, it may not have as much purchasing power in the future as it does today.

- **Asset/Product Allocation:** The investments and products you used when building your wealth are often not the best ones to use in retirement. Using the same mix can jeopardize your financial future.

- **Excess Withdrawal:** When you retire, you need to be mindful of how much you withdraw from your investments each year. A safe and sustainable withdrawal rate is the amount which can be taken from a portfolio with minimal probability of depleting the account during retirement.

- **Healthcare:** Longer lifespans and rising medical costs mean healthcare costs in retirement may be higher than you accounted for.

Your Retirement Income Plan

With these risks in mind, retirement is simply a new job: using your income sources to descend the mountain safely. To do so, you must address both the short-term challenge of needing money to live off of now, and the long-term challenge of growing and protecting your money for use later.

A good approach to creating a retirement income plan is using a *time-segmented strategy*. This strategy is based on the concept that you should not invest money you will use soon in the same way that you would invest money you do not need for 20 years.

This strategy lets you take advantage of this concept by investing more aggressively with money you do not need in the short-term while investing more conservatively with the money you will need sooner.

In one popular application of the time-segmented strategy, your money is divided into six segments, each lasting five years. Each segment holds assets ranging from very conservative to aggressive.

Money you will need in the first decade of retirement—the first two segments—is placed in safe, conservative investments. This gets you down the most treacherous part of the mountain safely.

Successive segments hold progressively more aggressive investments. Each segment is held for the longest period of time possible in order to achieve the best possible chance of excellent investing results. For each consecutive five-year period, subsequent segments are converted into the next lower-risk segment.

The time-segmented strategy is usually executed by setting up a unique account for each time segment. That way you know exactly what each account is for, when you will use it and what your strategy is for that portion of your money.

Your emotions are more easily managed because you know you have set aside money for your near future and you are not tempted to worry about wild stock market swings.

This approach can be customized to you and your goals and it allows you to plan according to your situation. It's simple, it plans for longevity, and it even allows you to give yourself pay raises to maintain your standard of living.

Structuring your time segments is both an art and a science. This is an area in which it is beneficial to work with a professional. The stakes for descending this part of the mountain are high.

Other Retirement Plan Options

As you research retirement income planning options, you will encounter several other common strategies. It's important that you understand each one before you choose. Here's an overview of what you are likely to see.

Put it in the Bank: This is like deciding to stay at the top of the mountain. It will give you safety—and you will safely go broke. Your money will barely grow and you will not be able to maintain your standard of living in retirement. You cannot live off of the interest alone, and if you take principal, you will quickly deplete your capital.

Buy a Guaranteed-Income Annuity: True to their name, guaranteed income annuities guarantee your income in retirement. That guarantee comes with a cost— *control*. If you use all of your life savings to buy an annuity, you will lose all control over your life savings.

Additionally, the annuity may not protect your spouse at the same level at which it protects you. And annuities do not often provide income increases which will allow you to maintain your standard of living in retirement.

Invest it All: This can grow your money and allow you to take a sustainable withdrawal (usually 4-6%) for your lifetime. But if you have poor investment returns during the first decade of your retirement, you are likely to run out of money with which to live.

This is jumping off the top of a mountain with a parachute. You are relying on luck to get you far enough away from the mountain so you can safely descend. But you do not want to rely on luck for the duration of your retirement. Advisors who recommend this method are keeping your money—and your retirement—at risk.

Your Retirement Plan Mantra

Regardless of which retirement plan strategy you pursue, you will do best if you ease into retirement. That does not mean you should keep working part time. It means you enter retirement without any preconceived notions of what your financial life will look like.

So, for the first part of your entry into retirement, your mantra should be *flexibility*. Embrace the ambiguity and keep your plans flexible. Delay making any irrevocable decisions. Don't be too eager to move into a new house or to relocate to a new part of the country.

Take the time to explore before you leap. Forget planning what you will spend down to the penny. Throw away your retirement itinerary. Rent a condo for a season before buying that new retirement house. Wait until you have settled into retirement before you begin planning how you will spend your time.

When you begin to prepare for retirement, find a financial Sherpa who is an expert at successfully guiding people down the mountain and into retirement.

APPENDIX A

WORKING WITH A FINANCIAL ADVISOR

I believe whether you do your own investing or work with a financial advisor, you can be successful. But there is a caveat: Investing on your own is like doing DIY repairs on your home. Some people can do them really well. For others, it can be a disaster and end up costing more than if they had hired a professional. The difference comes down to the homeowners' knowledge and experience.

According to a study by Vanguard, advisors can potentially add "about 3%" in net returns.[11] Like housing contractors, not all advisors are created equal. The person you have handling your financial future should be

---

11   Kinniry, Francis M., Colleen M. Jaconetti, Michael A. DiJoseph, Yan Zilbering, and Donald G. Bennyhoff. "Putting a Value on Your Value: Quantifying Vanguard Advisor's Alpha." Vanguard. September 2016. Accessed February 04, 2018. https://advisors.vanguard.com/iwe/pdf/ISGQVAA.pdf

as skilled as the person you would want to work on your home.

Ten Marks of a Good Financial Advisor

1. They should provide you with good advice covering a range of financial topics—not just investing.

2. They should help to reduce complexity and to simplify.

3. They should help you create a strategy and a plan for investing.

4. They should help you stay disciplined with your plan and process.

5. They should help you with asset allocation.

6. They should help you with investment selection.

7. They should help you with monitoring and rebalancing your portfolio.

8. They should discourage speculation with your serious money.

9. They should not try to predict stock market movements.

10. They should not make claims that they can beat the market while taking less risk.

Tips for Finding a Good Financial Advisor

If you want to find a good financial advisor, start by looking for a CFP® professional. CERTIFIED FINANCIAL PLANNER™ professionals are licensed, regulated and must take mandatory continuing education courses. CFP® professionals have to undergo rigorous training and endure strict oversight in order to retain the certification.

1. **Education**: CFP® professionals must develop their theoretical and practical knowledge by completing a course of study at a college or university offering a financial planning curriculum approved by the CFP® board.

2. **Examination**: CFP® professionals must pass a certification exam which tests their abilities to apply financial planning knowledge to real-life situations.

3. **Experience**: CFP® professionals must have several years of experience related to delivering financial planning services prior to earning the right to use the CFP® certification.

4. **Ethics**: CFP® professionals are held to the highest standards of ethics.

Even though CFP® professionals have undergone all of this training, there is still considerable variation among them. Investigate these five areas to see if a CFP® professional is someone you should trust with your investments.

1. **Ethics**: Above all, you need to know the person with whom you are working has your best interests at heart. Unfortunately, there is no sign that says, "Hey, here is a trustworthy advisor."—While the CFP® certification is a start, it is not perfect. You can find out if an advisor has ever been in trouble by viewing their individual record at FINRA's website. If you view the report and it has a red flag, read through the notes. A complaint about short-term market losses should be taken with a grain of salt and you should ask the CFP® professional about it before deciding. If the complaint is about serious matters such as a breach of ethics, look elsewhere for a financial advisor.

2. **Credentials**: The financial services industry has created many credentials that advisors use. Most of these credentials are worthless and are created for marketing purposes only. In my opinion, the industry only has a few credentials that really matter. The CFP® is one of them, and it represents the highest standard in financial planning. For information on the other certifications financial planners may have, go to FINRA.org. FINRA provides a list of all professional designations, along with the issuing organization, requirements, and accreditation associated with each designation.

3. **Experience**: How long have they been a financial advisor? With what type of clients do they work? Do they specialize in a certain area? You can learn this by

perusing their website and promotional materials, or by asking them directly.

4. **Philosophy**: What is their investing philosophy? Do they favor a strategic asset allocation, or do they believe in tactical strategies, quantitative investing or market timing?

5. **Process**: What is their investment process? How do they help you determine the best asset allocation and select individual investments? How do they go about rebalancing your investments to make sure you stick with the plan? How do they plan on communicating with you?

All of these are good questions to ask of your prospective financial advisor. There are also a few things people try to use to evaluate potential advisors which are not good indicators of how successful they will be with your portfolio.

1. **References**: Asking for references from a financial advisor you are considering will not help you. If you ask, you will be given a cherry-picked list of clients, none of whom will say anything critical about the financial advisor.

2. **Compensation Model**: The compensation model with which an advisor works does not correlate with their quality as an advisor. Good financial advisors will take care of you in any compensation system and bad

financial advisors will take advantage of you in any system.

A recent trend is to use "fee-based" compensation arrangements, wherein you are charged an annual fee based on a percentage of your account. These are popular with financial industry regulators because they are supposed to reduce the conflicts of interest by removing compensation based on the sale of an investment.

Fee-based-only compensation is not a complete model, because many financial products are not compatible with this system. Products such as annuities, life insurance, and disability insurance can be very important to your financial plan but have traditionally been available only in a commission-based model.

Both fee-based and commission-based models have their advantages and disadvantages. A third system, a hybrid of the two, gives your advisor the ability to manage your investments as a fiduciary, just like a fee-based model, but also gives them access to products that you may need as part of your financial plan. This is important, because it gives your advisor the most tools with which to help you while ensuring they have your best interests in mind.

3. **Performance**: Someone who asks about performance usually assumes that the advisor manages all their

clients' money in the same way. Even if your financial advisor tells you their three- or five-year return, it will be a misleading figure.

FREQUENTLY ASKED QUESTIONS

Question: Can I earn more than what my CDs are paying?

Answer: CDs have very little return relative to other investments because they take very little risk relative to other investments. Without taking on more risk, the CD saver cannot increase their return.

Additional Insight: You should consider what you are planning on using the money for. Remember: Your strategy should match your goal. If the money is for a short-term goal, you should stick with a short-term solution like a CD. If you are using CDs to try to solve a long-term challenge like saving for retirement or college, you are shortchanging yourself. If saving for a long-term goal, then you should consider a long-term investment strategy.

Question: I heard that the stock market is going to go down. Do you think I should sell now before it drops?

Answer: The stock market's short-term performance is completely unpredictable. If you sell your investments because you think they will go down in the short term, you are speculating, not investing. The market cannot be timed. Focus on your process and the results you are looking for will take care of themselves.

Additional Insight: Recall the story about Barron's Roundtable and how the best investors on Wall Street failed so miserably at predicting the near-term performance of the stock market. They have the best technology, training and skills, and they cannot accurately predict the market. Why would you be able to?

Question: I heard about an investment strategy which will let me time the market. What do you think?

Answer: See above. It will not work. Some strategies will work in the short-term, but they will inevitably fail over the long-term. Any success they do have is based completely on luck. Good investors do not rely on luck.

Additional Insight: It can be tempting to think we know what the stock market is going to do in the short run. Our brain works against us by using pattern recognition to make us think we can. The fact is that we simply cannot do it.

Question: I think the stock market is high right now. Does that mean it's not a good time to invest?

Answer: This thinking is just another form of market timing. It can work in the short run, but it will likely fail in the long term.

Additional Insight: Even the best investment strategy can experience losses in the short-term because of unlucky timing and chance. According to the previously mentioned study by Vanguard, if you invest in the stock market for one year, historically, your chance of losing money has been one in four. If you invested for 10 years, your chance of losing money has been one in 25. After 20 years, the chance of losing money drops to zero. Experiencing a negative return early in the investment lifespan is not uncommon, regardless of how good your investments are. [12]

Question: How much money do I need to save to retire?

Answer: This question is worthy of a book itself. Unfortunately, there is no one-size-fits-all answer.

Additional Insight: There is a better question than "How much money do I need when I retire?" It's "How much income do I need when I retire?" The amount of income your investments will need to provide in retirement depends on your income strategy, spending habits and how long you expect to live. From there, you can work backwards to how much you need to be setting aside each year for retirement.

---

12   "How Risk, Reward & Time Are Related." Vanguard. Accessed February 04, 2019. https://investor.vanguard.com/investing/how-to-invest/risk-reward-compounding.

Question: What is the stock market doing right now?

Answer: I don't keep track of the stock market's daily performance and neither should you.

Additional Insight: Today's news will be useless within hours—if it ever had any value. What good is information that is only good for a few hours, if you are planning for the next 20 years? Investors who focus on the daily performance of the stock market are focused on something over which they have no control. Focus instead on what you can control.

Question: My friend's 401(k) went up 17% last year and mine only went up 12%. What's up with that?

Answer: Your 401(k) and their 401(k) are probably not following the same strategy. Even if they are, the investments are probably different.

Additional Insight: Different strategies and levels of risk will yield different returns. If you are using the same strategy but different investments, you can experience differences in your return in the short-term. My advice would be to make sure that your 401(k) is set up specifically for you, for what you want to achieve and for what you are comfortable with. Don't worry about your friend's 401(k).

Question: Is gold a good investment?

Answer: Gold held as a small part of an overall investment strategy can be a good investment. Gold has shown some benefits as a diversification instrument, and it has hedging characteristics against inflation.

Additional Insight: Gold becomes popular whenever the stock market or the economy hits a rough patch. Some people think gold bypasses the risk/return principal, and that it never goes down. But gold does go up and down in value quite a bit. If you buy actual physical gold, you will only "experience" the fluctuation if you check the price of gold on a regular basis. If you buy gold certificates or gold-based investments which are actively traded, you would see those price changes reflected in your investments.

Question: Should I wait until after the election to see what's going to happen before I invest?

Answer: Despite what the financial news media would like you to think, the stock market has performed normally during election cycles over the last 40 years. Don't let them impact your investment process.

Additional Insight: Money and politics can both become emotionally-charged topics. Elections are difficult to predict. Over the long-term, the stock market continues to climb— regardless of who becomes president. People always find reasons to be uncertain, from Y2K, elections or the latest news of the day. The bad outcomes people expect usually never come.

Question: Should I invest in Bitcoin or another cryptocurrency?

Answer: Buying Bitcoin is a speculation, not a real investment. It is fine to buy it, but do not treat it as an investment.

Additional Insight: If you must buy Bitcoin, treat it like gambling. Limit how much you want to put into it, separate that money from your serious investments and imagine that you have already lost it. If you win big, great.

THE 10 COMMANDMENTS OF INVESTING

This is an invaluable cheat sheet for your investing. If you find yourself not following one of the commandments on these pages, re-examine how you invest and adjust accordingly.

Alternatively, speak with a financial advisor about how you can get back on track.

1. **Listen to Wisdom and Ignore Information.** The noise coming from the market will only distract you from your investing strategy.

2. **Use the Right Timeframe for Your Goal.** Long-term goals require long-term investments; short-term goals require short-term investments.

3. **Do not try to Beat or Time the Market.** Both are losing games for private investors. Be content with the returns the market gives you.

4. **Do Take on Appropriate Amounts of Risk.** Regardless of your goal's time frame, you need to be able to beat inflation in order to achieve a return.

5. **Diversify by Asset Class and Sector.** Never put all your eggs in one basket. If it breaks, so will all your eggs.

6. **Have a Strategy and Execute It.** Develop a strategy based on sound principles, then execute it by investing regularly.

7. **Value Simple Processes.** Complexity usually reduces or eliminates returns.

8. **Speculate Responsibly.** If you must speculate, never use more than 10% of your portfolio and never top up your speculating account.

9. **Focus on what you can Control.** Focusing on anything else is a waste of time and will cost you returns.

10. **Re-train Your Internal Biases.** Work to govern your emotions so you do not trade based on them. Always fall back on your investing values and strategy.

ABOUT THE AUTHOR

CHRIS MERCHANT
CFP® BFA®

C hris Merchant is a CERTIFIED FINANCIAL PLANNER™ and Behavioral Financial Advisor™. He holds an MBA and has received various industry awards throughout his professional career, including the 2019 Women's Choice Award® for Financial Advisors.

He has developed a unique ability and passion for helping other people realize their potential while instilling confidence in endeavors they once thought impossible or unachievable. This ability is strengthened by his capacity to analyze very complex problems and turn them into step-by-step, easily followed solutions.

He founded Hunt Country Wealth Management, LLC with his wife and business partner, Heather. Hunt Country Wealth Management is an independent financial planning and wealth management firm that works with individuals throughout Virginia's Hunt Country, Northern Virginia, and the Shenandoah Valley. They specialize in fee-based financial planning, in-house investment management, and income solutions for the growing retiree population.

Chris uses the principles, methods, and strategies he has laid out in this book for his clients. If you would like a free consultation to discuss your financial situation, please contact their office. (https://huntcountryinvestments.com)

DISCLOSURE PAGE

All guarantees referenced are based on the claims paying ability of the issuing company.

The Women's Choice Award® Financial Advisor Program by WomenCertified Inc. is a recognition program for advisors who provide quality service and strong commitment to their female clients.

Advisors who qualify for the Award are evaluated using 17 objective criteria: 1) Clientele are at least one-third women or male-female couples; 2) Accepting new clients; 3) Actively employed as a licensed or credentialed professional in financial services for a minimum of three years; 4) Credentials include an IAR (Investment Advisory Representative), a FINRA-registered advisor/broker, an RIA (Registered Investment Advisor), a CPA (Certified Public Accountant), CFP® (Certified Financial Planner), PFS (Personal Financial Specialist), or a licensed attorney practicing in financial services; 5) Must be in compliance with regulatory requirements of the SEC, state securities regulators in states where they do business, and self-regulatory bodies; 6) Must be in good standing with the standards of the firm with which they are affiliated; 7) Must have a favorable regulatory and complaint history and who sign an affidavit to that effect*; 8) Must not have been subject to a regulatory action that resulted in their license being suspended or revoked, or payment of a fine; 9) Must not have been convicted of a felony; 10) Must not have filed for personal bankruptcy in the past ten years; 11) Assets under management; 12) Number of clients (households) served by the advisor; 13) The advisor's client retention rate over a three-year period;

14) How many firms the advisor has been associated with in the past ten years; 15) The advisor's education and professional designations; 16) Educational programs and events provided for clients; and 17) The advisor's record of community service. In addition to the criteria and to augment the evaluation process, the advisor is required to submit letters of validation from senior representatives at their respective firm or broker dealer and/or they may have completed a survey of the advisor's clients to obtain client feedback regarding service and practices. The first 10 criteria are required, while the last 7 are considered in determining qualification. *A favorable regulatory and complaint history is defined by WomenCertified, Inc. as no more than three customer complaints filed against them with any regulatory authority, no individual contributions to a financial settlement regarding a filed customer complaint, and no suspension or revocation of license as the result of a regulatory action.

The award may not be representative of any one client's experience. The award is not indicative of the advisor's future performance. Financial advisors do not pay a fee to be considered or placed on the final list of Women's Choice Financial Advisor Award®, though they may have paid a basic program fee to cover the cost of comprehensive review and client survey.

Made in the USA
Middletown, DE
08 June 2022

66860264R00066